WERE
THERE
GAZELLE
LAURA K. MCRAE

For Shona –
May your journeys
bring joy and wonderful
visions

Laura

PEDLAR PRESS | ST. JOHN'S

WERE
THERE
GAZELLE

LAURA K. MCRAE

Laura K McRae

COVER ART   Myriam Rousseau, *GAZELLE I*, 2019
DESIGN   Mark Byk
TYPEFACES   Leo Book and Stern Pro
Printed in Canada at Coach House Printing, Toronto ON

LIBRARY AND ARCHIVES CANADA CATALOGUING IN PUBLICATION
Were there gazelle / Laura K. McRae.
McRae, Laura K., 1966- author.

Poems.
Canadiana 2019019605X | ISBN 978-1-8971-41-99-1 (softcover)

I. TITLE.

LCC PS8625.R334 W47 2020 | DDC C811/.6—DC23
First Edition

ACKNOWLEDGEMENTS
The publisher wishes to thank the Canada Council for the Arts and the NL Publishers Assistance Program for their generous support of our publishing program.

Contents

Each landscape leaves its mark—
a scratch at the heart, faint
as a pole-scar on talus,

sunk like a bootprint in tundra.

—Elena Johnson

I

The Dead Are Dead

Bones of the Cathedral

i.

We huddle over a wind-scraped pool—
night on Dettah Ice Road. White ice
above black compresses

the living river.

We cannot see the lines
in the hand of the lake.

ii.

Sitting on the crest, San Gabriel Mountains,
in the oyster-grey ashes

of day. The wail of a single peacock
trails into silence.

We fry pancakes as an owl of fog
ghosts across the gloaming.

iii.

We wander in the shadow of Little Green Mountain.
Astroturf drapes dark clay lining a new grave.

The mountain's greens:
emerald, malachite.

Not the sea's lucent jade,
bluing the pitch-dark depths, but clear—

like your eyes.

iv.

We are all travellers, no flaming swords here.

We carry food—bread, milk, almond, honey—
take ship, laden with purpose.

Enter these woods, walk into the night.

v.

Maunder between stones—aunt,
great-uncle, great-great-grandmother.

Your grandfather lies in Macedonia
under a grassy slope. Goats graze there,
the marker crumbles.

vi.

Three ravens, black as calligraphy ink,
burnished tide on a cloudless night.

Their kill bleeds across snow.

Skull blanched and picked clean,
the dusted white of juniper berries.

vii.

They moved the bodies,
loaded them on trucks, carted them
to a new plot in a new state.

My grandfather slid out; I picture him
careening back to town,

to the place he had lain.

viii.

Tomorrow will be everywhere; we just have to wait.

We think the body will remain
forever where it was, but

it will probably just drop,
leaden, to the highway.

ix.

The bones of the cathedral are vanished,
only hooves and nails, hair, remain.

In the end, we are unmoored from
all we know. Three ravens

crouch in snow,
rise to perch on the streetlight,

trigger the warming lamp.

I Listen to Istanbul

I listen to Istanbul, intent, eyes closed,

the lilt of Turkish wafting on smoke
shredded from lips of hookahs,

growling burr of the call to prayer
rising like sun-smoke from pavement

on hottest days. It colours spaces between trees,
marigolds in deep shade.

Istanbul sings in the cant of merchants,

the sway of lamps suspended
from arched ceilings, the whisper

of a rug sliding from a waist-high stack. You
flip it onto a hyacinth-veined floor. Istanbul

hums in the blue sky, the minarets white
in noon's flat light.

Istanbul calls in the susurrating tide of the Bosphorus,

cabs sliding through narrow alleys. We stop for thick coffee,
rosewater jelly dusted with powder.

We slip under a cool vault,
the haze of mingled breath lingering above our heads.

I listen to Istanbul, intent, eyes closed,
the sliver of moon rising over rooftops.

I listen to the dark night of Istanbul.

Were There Gazelle: Sacrifice

An aircraft comes to rest on the stony perimeter.
A gazelle pivots. Desert to either side sketched with

red earth, scrub, cacti. This is a summer of sacrifice
and anything can happen. She darts,

tangents the swooping highway. No rooftops,
no vantage point, only a buzzard looping

the sky. I watch from the Mustang. On my radio,
the bridge of "Hotel California."

Her hindquarters bunch, erupt.
White streak in the expanding distance.

Village in Kerala

Insects too, as permanent as skin,
cloud the air. We crawl the main road.

Dust rises fine and red,
not from our wheels,

but from behind the lumbering elephant,
elderly, forehead white-painted.

Women pass in their white saris
gold banding bright in the dusk.

On one side, a housewares shop
piled high with boxes and metal

tools; on the other, a shrine—
to Nandi, perhaps, or Shiva. Marigold garlands

trail from railings. Further on, a church.

The chatter of monkeys follows us,
our tires eat the slope.

The Sun Casts No Shade

The sun casts no shade at noon;
it is always noon in Tangier. The kasbah's rusted

white surrenders to *bluespinksyellows*
of the medina, glare of narrow alleys.

And when the minarets swallow the sun, the medina
pulls closed its doors. It is the time of the *zocco chico*,

where Bowles might have shared a glass with Burroughs
in the sudden twilight. Stein nursed a brandy and soda

in that same brindled light, on a high balcony
where men still lean over mosaic tables. These asphalt streets

still tunnel into the kasbah, but here no Hemmingway
tamps his pipe, no Wharton sips her drink in the fall of night.

Here the spirits wear *djellaba*, buy olives, greens from
the Berber women, listen for the call to prayer.

How to Know When the Dead Are Dead

Firefly points flicker from cut bronze over
the white walls and crenellated roofs of Fes.

The city spreads north, a suggestion of silence
until voices rise from the dusk and Arabic

splashes in the courtyard fountain. No horns,
no engines. Just houses lit from within.

If I could photograph time,
I would capture this rooftop moment

when the eighth century meets the twenty-first:
olives, oranges, crumbling plaster,

clean dung of mules. Old lanterns
flash electric signals at the horned moon.

This moment will vanish before the shudder of generators,
high-rises, wide windows open to the view,

motorcycles in the souk where donkeys carry cages of cocks.
They crow in the lamplight, thinking for a moment it is dawn.

Evening in Toronto, August, 2013

We sit silhouetted by candlelight.
There may be stars, a waning moon,

but we are drawn by white china and
a single stem of orchids in a mason jar.

I tilt my head toward the mill, a warble
of water over stone. But a passing car

turns my ear back to the table, to the clatter
of cutlery, the waiter. Seamus Heaney

died today, and voices in the twilight
are enough.

Twilight in New Orleans

Minted tumblers sweat in our palms,
quinine prickle of tonic
cuts thick velvet of magnolia.

The rumbling bass that floods Bourbon Street
can't be Louis Armstrong's. Mother said she met him in the fifties,
but she said so many things. Smoke bruises my cheek,

and I can see the girl's face in her cigarette's
ember, too young for the night.

This Is Fes

Sun whites the alleyway. On its washed
        stones, the sharp line of paint, falcon, star,
        black diagonal slash—each traced
dark on white plaster. No posters,

no toothy smiles, no coiffed hair. The parties
        ebb and flow. The symbols
        come and go with the wheeling of the sun,
the cycles of the moon.

A month later, at home, blanket across knees,
        a political advertisement,
        all white teeth and pressed suit
across my screen—

a wall, yes,
        a way.
        Sprayed paint to tell
you who you are.

Were There Gazelle: Waiting

Was that a gazelle I saw clear a fallen
log, seek refuge in the hills, plough

through the swell of grass? Was it the shadow
of some raptor trawling the plains for spoils?

Did a gazelle pause on tender hooves,
print the tiny half moons of her passing

in soft red earth? Dust
clouds grass. Tears streak my gaze.

Atchafalaya Basin, Louisiana, May 1986

Later she will search her skin for the bloom of dirt
and supple bodies of leeches,

but now she wades in the muck, each step
a skirmish against the suck of mud. Her t-shirt

straggles over hiking shorts, proclaims
Atchafalaya the *Gator Capitol of Louisiana.*

The camera around her neck lists, telephoto lens
drawing it down, into the bayou. Palms cradle

metal, and she raises it to her eye—
an egret lights on a submerged log,

plunges its beak into the water,
emerges in a flash of silver. In the background,

amid splintered trunks of cypress,
a single gilded iris emerges from the water,

a lotus rising from the muck
to bloom.

Encounter

Yes, she is pleased to have the man take her picture,
stands in the wind-whipped frame, hair salt-strewn,
sand plastered across her cheek. See,

she is burnt across nose, ear-tips,
cheekbones. Her knees pebbled,
cotton shirt creased. The sun behind her

shadows her face, hair a bright orb. A dog
snatches his frisbee from the air, arc of spray
from his legs. The man releases

the shutter, gentles the film from the trap door,
watches her face, the surf, watches the dog
appear in the black square. He hands

her the photo, crimps a few dollars, walks away.

The Find

She is a long-necked bird, bending
toward the water, dabbling beak fingers

in the tide pool. Her first dip nets a scallop,
shell purpled with the tide.

The next brings up polished driftwood—her wrist
sags with the weight. She turns it over and over, catching

the light. Her cocked crane's head, her long
crane limbs. She trawls again, pulls up

a jet oval tumbled by waves, a fine profile
outlined on the cameo's battered face.

Some lost passenger bore it into the sea.
Now taken in, washed of sand, it is all that remains.

One Night in Buda

Lamps on the chain bridge light Danube's ribbon
under a circular trace of moon. Bluffs swell overhead;

Parliament's dome glows amber. Its reflection
ripples in the wake of a barge.

A lone bird plummets across the hemisphere, wings pointed,
and the flock follows, a blanket snapped and thrown.

I do not know these are not starlings. That they are geese
dwarfed by distance and that enormous vault. Next morning,

I remember them infinitely small, wingbeats muffled by miles.
I throw bread to wheeling gulls, wince

at their raucous cries, my face buffeted by soft feathers.
I peer across the Danube through pied flaxen light.

Monastery, Sinaia, Romania

Roses with no blooms, just the last
shriveled petals reflected in well water.

Wooden cross, windows with diamond panes,
stone cornices. Each wall painted, pigment on stone.

The torsos are clear, landscape too,
but the heads are rubbed grey, de-faced.

Only their aureoles mark them as human—
and the human hands folded before them.

On bald floors, I imagine carpets,
silk printed with centuries of dust

cast from feet, some reverently bare,
others booted as they enter sacred space.

In the distance, I can just hear water,
a clot of traffic, a single horn.

Today is still distant, but the park,
the walled garden, cannot bar its voice.

Ten Days in Beijing

Acres of concrete, no grass, before the Hidden City.
Curved cornices, mythic beasts, phoenix, dragon—yin to yang.

Bi xi, the dragon-tortoise, carved in soft wood, burnished
with beeswax. Mothers dangle infants between knees.

The Drum Tower holds great barrelled vessels; we climb
knee-high steps in the great gong of wet heat.

Rickshaws criss-cross the *hutong*, double gates
deny houses. A plastic basin is home to a tiny turtle.

A fine stream of tea glides into porcelain cup, trays of sweets,
Hello Kitty in the shop window.

The Temple of Heaven is formed of stacked cylinders.
In the grounds, elderly men play *mah jong*.

A hundred years from today, the Temple will still stand,
new wood, new paint, but we will agree it is the same, and

mah jong tiles will click in the fingers
of new old men.

Were There Gazelle: No Chances

A gazelle, body unfurled in the moment of flight,
here on this scrubby sickle between sea

and sea. She clears shale foundations, pivots,
then hooves contact sand, and she streaks across the wash,

incoming flood filling cobbled pools beneath
her feet. To either side, the ocean

surges to full, seaweed marbling the drink.

There are no chances here, only moon and tide,
grass flattened by the storm.

A Fox, a Dog in the Mist

Anger is a fox curled in the cave of your chest, eyes
flashing flame, burden teased by bubbles of laughter.

The cave is the colour of the sea—darkness
soaking the foot of a granite precipice.

Memories snarl as you sip, madness in the evening sun.
She steps on cautious feet, the fox. Claws scar clay

as she scrabbles through brush. The city is not for her,
and she slinks, flattened to earth, toward green bins,

pelt matted with grass and motor oil.
She sips from rusty puddles and endures.

There is no fox. Just a cave of anger
and a distant dog in the mist.

Morning at Summer Palace, Beijing

Fog rises off the lake to bury the sun. Its steel gleam glints off
willows that dip their feathered fingers in the shallows.

In the distance, a man balances on his pontoon,
pole and hook poised to loop fronds of weed.

Granite walkways steam in the heat, and as I turn down
a path to the Fragrance Tower and the Marble Boat,

an old man with his long-handled sponge
paints a new line with water: *Heart Sutra*.

The opening lines dry and fade
as he draws the final characters.

I continue on the path,
and he begins to write again.

I See China

Sky, mist, a peak mingle in the mid-ground.
Light glows from the background, a halo of white, peach.

In the foreground, the ruins of piers, flitting seabirds.
They seek sanctuary on the broken teeth of the mooring.

Left, foregrounded, the boat. Its reflection wavers in the water.
The Blue Rigi is in Switzerland, but the boat says China,

the Summer Palace, the wash of sun on grass,
dragon boats tracing watery rings

on the lake's tablet. I've never been to Switzerland,
never seen the Blue Rigi rise beyond that lake.

I see only the Summer Palace on that canvas.

Ring of Brodgar, Orkney

My face behind the camera, my lens aimed
past his expectant face. I twist the black cylinder
and he emerges in the foreground, shoulder

propped against one Brodgar stone. In the distance,
a figure: jeans, cotton shirt with white shell buttons,
collar crawling down the back, perhaps blue once.

Spade plunges into straw-stippled turf, rises,
is poised to strike again. To the left, the marbled
stretch of Stenness, curve of the farm road

across the fields to Maeshowe. At the top, a tern,
wings clipped by the instant of the shutter.

Village at Birsay

The tide is out, a hand drawn back from a face,
revealing lines of the strand.
I stoop, pluck a ribbon of seaweed and
finger a coil of shell as I cross along the seabed.

I climb crumbling shale to an expanse of shore
and the scent of dry hay. From here the village walls
stand inches high, built slab-on-slab. I trace outlines of the hall,
largest rectangle in that clustered map, and smaller houses,

each squared with a low threshold where a door once hung.
Norsemen worked here. The women carded wool and wove,
children streaming along the shore, chasing puffins
that bumbled through the grass. The sea begins to rise.

I consult the table tucked in my pocket, think of those
caught by storm, the unexpected turn of tide.
I cross to Mainland just as the seabed is washed by waves,
the rocky headland an island once more.

Were There Gazelle: Delta

Water gleams at the bayou's source,
whiff of rust, rotting cilantro. A possum,

eyes jet beads in the shadows, mewls a protest,
teeth a mountain range in the valley of his jaw.

He climbs a convenient birch, nails
savaging the living tree. A gazelle

lopes through the mossy wood, lifts forelegs,
then flanks, over a fallen cypress, melts

into the undergrowth. Watery sun clings
to moist skin, day tangles the frayed cuffs of my jeans.

White surf stirs the bayou's pelt,
then it's a gator sliding off a log into

the dingy water. If he floats south
long enough, he'll reach the briny waters of the gulf.

Tail's white flash, hint of hoof, a twilight
mirage. Unseen, cicadas drone

in the shadows, and a dragonfly noses an iris
lifted just above the waterline—or could it be

a hummingbird, that touch of colour almost lost
in the emerald rust of jungle?

A jewelled bird, lighting the forest?   /41

II

It's a Far Cry

It's a far cry to Delhi—
Dilli dur ast—

cork green and brown, and the hills, staggered in the distance,
capped with temples, cream in the far mist. We drive through
morning's false dawn. Wild pigs, hoary and broad, scuttle into
underbrush among the crows.

The first steps are shallow and easy. We clamber upward until
our breath catches in our throats—*Five hundred steps, only three
thousand more*—my eyes film. Dust in my mouth, I lean against a
wall, gulp air into screaming lungs. The long stair stretches metres,
makes it feel easy. A ten-inch rise changes everything, and the
burning again. *Where are you from?—Canada—I've done this five
times today. You'll be fine.*—I watch a sling chair. Porters climb
easily, pass. I look down at my feet, try to find the swinging rhythm
of the porters.

A raptor swoops, and I wonder at the joy, the ease. I see blue velvet
bloom rose and gold,

a far cry—

It's a far cry to Delhi as velvet night fades and the call to prayer
snakes through the morning hush, rising, falling. This is not the
low drone of Fes, the ululating wail of Istanbul. It is dark, light,
a lush strand of cobalt shifting through dawn's flushed bloom.

Parrots perch, flutter past windows in smoky light. Hawks soar.
We hold our breath as they hover weightless,

that far cry to Delhi—

Brittania Café, berry pilau. *Do you know Hillary? Tell her,*
when you get back. Tell her... He runs his eye around the over
full dining room, the mezzanine. *I will, if I get the chance.*
He hands me another letter, laminated, this one from the Queen.
I'm ninety-two this year. My son will carry on when I'm gone.
I spoon another taste of pilau, the recipe Iranian, this moment
on a Mumbai corner—

Houseboat, low sides, wooden benches, cloth awning sagging
slightly above our heads. The air, heavy with water, redolent of cut
and rotting grass.

The laundry white as it sprawls on the bank. She stands shin deep
in the river, bungalow behind her.

We pass a shrine, white fence, marigolds dangling like suns on
strings, fabric mangled in her hands. On the shore, a line of
washing, basket waiting.

We pass a shrine, white fence, marigolds small suns winking at
the bright ball above. She lies in the water, legs floating up, bare in
river's wash.

We pass a shrine, white fence, marigolds setting suns against the
green. Laundry, bannering white and red in the steamy air.

We pass a shrine—

The grass, the riverbank alive with snakes. One rises and mantles, hisses, fangs extended, head darting from the long stretch of body. Another submits, head ducking into wrapped coils. The bank silent, the water spreads behind us. We loose our moorings, push into the lake.

I still watch my feet, each nook, watch for scaly loops, deep-slitted eyes, tucked behind the couch, under my Toronto bed when I get up in the night.

It's a far cry from the Delhi of my dreams. Highway suspended above shacks, raw planks, corrugated tin roofs. They stretch east and west until they give way to the highrises and broad avenues of New Delhi. Palisades girdle lawns shaded with fruit trees. Outside their confines, banyans and more shacks: plywood, paper, corroding metal. Men cook on charcoal braziers, sell coconuts as we pass. They chop off their wooden heads, and we sip from the bowl.

Banyans drop their roots, spread their broad branches. This is not the great banyan of Kerala—here in Mumbai, photos of swamis are tacked along cratered trunks. Marigolds trail on strings, but the air lies grey and gritty, dust on a pigeon's wing, not the dappled gold of Kerala.

Like dust on a pigeon's wing is the gritty cloak shrouding Delhi.
Dung fires, the expirations of nine million souls, dust of cows
shuffling through careening tuk-tuks, a pandemonium of parrots,
brilliantly emerald and euphoric among the trees.

The buoyant leaves of Munnar drift, loosed from their fragile joints.
They fall to lie glittering on rolling acres of tea. We spiral up, above
the plantations to the hilltops, rock larded with gorse and tall
grasses swaying like dancers, music whispering as arms brush arm.

Arm brushes arm, feet shuffle on pavement, the sun is a hammer on the anvil of our heads.

Buy a postcard, book of photos?—No. I want this moment like clear light behind my eyes in the blaze of sun on marble domes. The Taj is never dim. Across the river, a young bride holds thumb and forefinger in a pincer—her photo will show her plucking the temple from its gardens.

The sky is a pigeon's wing, grey and iridescent, a black pearl lit from within.

It's a far cry to this black pearl, lit from within, Palitana atop
its peak. But we are below in the valley, its long single street.
Spangled fabrics hang from shop walls, and the woman cries
BAM BAM, reaches forward with clawed fingers. Her teeth are stained
with *paan*, and she follows us chanting. This is her road, her town.
Does she climb to Palitana? Does she look to the mountain?

In the soft blush of evening—stars, no lights in the valley—we can smell pepper from the trees below, the taut slap of clay from my bungalow as we climb the hill. The okra is crisp and flavoured with cumin, *pittu* a rough tube of starch. We swill *chai*, set our mugs on the red-and-white-checkered cloth, plastic muttering with our movement.

In the distance, monkeys skirmish among the leaves. I imagine cobras in the undergrowth, mice, beetles grubbing in warm earth.

It's a far cry to this divot in the road. Vegetable huts line the asphalt,
canvas roofs taut against the harsh glare of sun. Cars
and trucks tarry, caught by their own numbers. This is a place
of males only. Boys dart and weave along the road.

A tiny child flings himself forward—trucks scream to a stop, cars
lurch—silence. They carry him, head hanging over a broad shoulder,
through the dust. Painted lorries grind

                                        into that far cry—

It's a far cry to Delhi, the streets alive with rambling cows grazing
on mowed median, forming new traffic circles. Tuk-tuks slither
around cars, cars slide past vans, and vans zoom beyond trucks—
a vast anthill.

I wonder what it looks like to three parrots soaring overhead.
I wonder what it looks like to the rats quarreling in the roots of
a banyan, lonely in a traffic median.

In Bhavnagar, cows walk to work with the shopkeepers, crop the
unclaimed grass, donate milk for whole families. Everyone wheels
around them.

I rest my hand on a warm flank. The head swings, and a huge eye
blinks at me, swings back to the grass.

.

In the blazing sun of Mattancherry, streets turn and turn, lead us deeper into the quarter. There the synagogue with its pressed glass lamps, its carved railings, carpets along the ancient hardwood, the central ark.

We sit softly, breathe centuries of incense, look to the Star of David. They say only six remain of the hundreds who first came here. The rest have gone to Israel.

Do they miss the high Kerala sun? The winding streets? The lilt of Malayalam floating on the breeze, seeds to the hushed wind?

A muted breeze floats its seeds, and Nandi there in the courtyard, hewn from black basalt, legs tucked, blanket across his back. White plaster curls its hand around the inner court, gate open, releasing the stone patio, strands of marigold drape the door posts. Smooth pillars rise—

It's a far cry to the shore, to the fly of fishing net. They tip the weight. It sinks deep then rises, weighted by salt water and their small catch. They scoop out silvery bodies, toss them to shore.

We move along, sea on our right, road on the left, past the vendor with the day's catch. He beckons us, grates cabbage for *thoran*— *It's my own design*—We buy six, for us, for friends. He wraps them in slight paper. We move along.

We make *thoran* back in Toronto, crisp with cabbage and carrot, accompanied by steaming *pittu*, sambar, fried okra. We are back in Kerala, eating under the night sky, the fitful tide of our music.

The photograph is vibrant, but the green has faded, parrots in
shadow, the emerald flicker of their movements stilled. The dust
doesn't rise with my footsteps, and that scent of scrub and dung
is replaced by hand sanitizer's sharp sting. The deep carving on the
red sandstone is muted, flat. I can no longer see the figures
or their obliterated faces. I have no photograph of the long gully
with its ruined walls—

                                    a far cry—

III

Distributaries

and the headlamps
gleam,
touch the streaked windshield,

soothe that crack from my four-year-old
head, an incision
poorly stitched, improperly

healed.   That golden beam
picks out exhausted remains
of factories, broken heads

of dinosaurs. The road is blanketed in fog
that muffles the lines, incisions

beautifully stitched
and fully healed, and the light
is the glow from a bedside lamp

                                        and I imagine
Venice   the canals, water
lipping tin cans and cigarette butts
against high stone walls.   Gondolas

drift past that place
where the safe fell through floor

after floor
into pooling water
in *The Italian Job*.   It's nothing like

                              this salt-scoured place
where puffins nestle in storm-carved cradles
and every prehistoric tomb hosts

                         chomping sheep.
In this vast north
frostbite is only legend, shiny celluloid,

packing plastic—   push
the bubbles until they backfire

                    like a car
on those nights
when silence is black fleece.

Have you ever
noticed the eye of a fish? Guts

sprawling on crimson
ice, a porthole, a dime—

                                        gleaming.
Nobody rides horses anymore.
In Texas it's cars—Trans Am, Camaro,
Mustang—

long hood slinks from curt back,
low slung, grip the road with

                        rubber fingers
rollick the range   nibble the dust
the roadrunner speeding away

from the coyote,
legs a blurred wheel.

I saw one in the desert   *Geococcyx californicus*
a lifetime ago

                    but it was Arizona
that evening in the desert
when the sun dipped to the horizon, lit

manzanita
firing them in the distance—
Moses's burning bush.   In our white Toyota,

no air, no radio
wheels a furred disc,
we crossed the desert at twilight,

                    stars
cracked ice in the breathless
air, and mirages woven

                        through a warp of mesquite.
Chargers gallop into battle, and Travolta
guns his engine under the Sixth Street bridge,

                              skirts the narrow
L.A. River ribbon and feeds his Mustang
as we fed our steeds, curries it with moleskin,

tools tires like hooves.
                        The Stanley steamer
charged on wood and water. Push a hose
over the side, hope you siphon

water, not the east Texas swamp, fuel it
like the old African Queen,

Bogart in the waist,
dry wood for a finicky engine. Now

we burn gasoline, smoke the same
grey-black
                    and pungent.

It billows like the dust of hooves galloping,

                     wide wheels
hug asphalt. A skull lies beside the road

                          a Georgia O'Keefe
the colour of the concrete slab
where the laugh house once stood,
round, littered with desiccated fruit,

the colour of the calla lilies
in that Diego Rivera nude.

                          I bought a replica
at Frida Kahlo's home in Mexico—the blue
walls, the garden, green-spangled, and the painted
woman
                    her back streaked olive, arms curved

                                in embrace.
Calidity is like that, clouds rising
on the horizon. They say the heat

is an anvil,
but that's the desert—the hammer
falls on roadrunners,

groundhogs, the skulls
of the dead and chests
of the dying.
                    Like Hephaestus,

artisan of the gods,
whose anvil rings with the weapons
he fashions, Thor's hammer—

Chris Hemsworth or *The Prose Edda*—
gods die and
Ragnarok hovers at the edge

                    of vision.
But here I imagine an axe,
the deep ring
of steel slicing heartwood,

the rhythm of Bunyan's blade
as he sweeps trees aside.
But this is not the Pacific Northwest,

and rain won't cool, mist won't cloud
out the sun.
                    This is the great gong

                              of heat.
They say if you put a frog in water,
slowly bring it to boil,

the frog won't notice, won't
save itself. But when we
slide into the shimmering swelter

that hovers
above the asphalt floors

                    of the Forbidden City
there is no place to jump, no horse
to saddle

                    no trees,
no grass, and the buildings—wood
gilded fantastical, pitched

roofs—offer
no greater shade than the graphite skies.

Have you ever sketched a cauldron?
Yourself floating in it,

but the water over the fire
cool, icebergs
afloat in the steam, and you,

destined
to come to grief on those sharp,

                    crystalline edges?
When you cross the desert
at night, the sky is rent
with the eyes of sheep,

the swirling gold of moon
and stars
Van Gogh's *Starry Night*.

The vast expanse
                    presses
into the roof, the hood
of the Toyota and the boxed air,

humid with recycled breath,
spliced with petrol and the rasp

of orange peel.

                    And I wonder
about the cowboys who rode shrouded
under the black fleece of night, breath

mingling
with the rumbling breath of their steeds,

horses' eyes portals
that reflect the moon, dimes

                              gleaming.
That same moon is clipped
by the trunks of sequoias, veiled

by a mantle of myrtlewoods
that grow only in Oregon. They pepper
the north California coast

Umbellularia californica
                    but no one
thinks of them—there they are laurel,
pepperwood, cinnamon bush, headache

                    tree. Their wood
glows golden, its honeyed light
daubed with fingerprints

                    of giants.
But cedar grows in the corner of
the old cemetery. That mossy angle was once

the far field of the farm. The daughter
of the house died—scarlet fever—
and they buried her

in that secluded nook,
wooden cross with her name
cut deep in pine.

The next family laid their grandmother
next to her under the bloom of needles—
another pine cross

                    another name carved deep.
My great-grandfather is there—
his wife
            his children and parents

now rest there too.
The young husband lies

                            under stone.
They lost track of his parents, mowed
down those wood crosses. My father says
he remembers them

                          though he could not
read the names.   There's a space
beside my mother, space
on her stone for Father's name.

And the raw lines of text
will round
                    will soften
with the years in the green-mottled

Oregon rain.
                    In the far north
of Scotland, rain does not glow that strange

peridot-touched jade. It streams, the color
of iris stalks along the horizon, slanting

into the sea.
It splinters across the leaves of the rowan
Rosaceae sorbus—the witch tree,

mountain ash, quicken tree, Quickbeam,
Ent of Rowan shape

in Tolkien's epic—
standing lone like the Norse first woman
crafted from its branches.

One island
hosts a lone tree. It grips
the rocks but leans
far out to sea, dropping its leaves

to float
small boats
for some errant mouse, some Thumbelina
adrift in the restless waves

                                        and I imagine
Bornholm, unmoored in the Baltic,
and Hammerhaus, round

stone towers brooding
over broken surf at the quarry,
over Vang curving along the shoreline

                                        to the south.
The village saw the iron age, greeted
the Vikings.
                        They must have wondered

at a fortress
commanding the sea.
                        The Vikings
named that white-capped stretch

Whale Road
                        watery trails
marked by moonlight, the moon

a slice of fruit, half
glowing above
                        its twin and opposite
quartered into the sea, decanting its wake

                into the waning tide.
The waters draw back
from Birsay's tidal plain, retreat,

expose firm sand marked
by troughs of waves. Our feet
make no mark

on that floor.
                Waters

                                  surge

into bayous, splinters

of sea
                        injected
into the silt-rich delta.
Then the tide draws back, gulps

verdant water
from the soft river mouth. Heron fish

in the brackish waters, pull pike
from among submerged logs, the roots

                                    of cedars.
There seems to be no tide
in the Mediterranean, evaporation
exceeds precipitation.

                          Cool water
streams in
through the Straits of Gibraltar
and circulates

through the Roman *Mare Nostrum*,
Akdeniz, al Bahr. When you stand
on a rooftop in Tangier's kasbah,

you can look across that cyan stretch
streaked with sapphire and the pale
wash of hyacinths

and see Spain.

Matisse, in the Grande Café de Paris—
in Tangier,
not Texas, not France—painted

square, white buildings,
delphinium sky. Those canvases
never show the street—vendors

line the tunnelling passages.
The shoe seller's stall is a forest
of slippers—leather and embroidered

silk, the russet of cinnabar, tumeric,
saffron, the drab of cork
leaves, Tyrian purple, true indigo.

But Chaouen,
Chaouen is blue, Tuareg blue, the walls,
the sky, the water that rushes down

the Rif. Chefchaouen, city of the two horns,
Ashawen, *Xauen*. Hike up from the kasbah
to the fabric sellers

and shake out the folds
of the *djellaba*, run a finger
along cactus-embroidered seams.

The walls lean inward, cut
off the sun, the sky
obscured by scarves—cotton, sabra

silk, the finest wool—flags
tangled by a breeze. Under
that fabric dome, you cannot see

the hills,
you cannot see the High Atlas range
stretch forth its arms

                    to embrace Fes.
Do you wake in the deep night
to sparks of colour behind
closed eyes? Do they

resolve into keyhole
doorways, piles
of star-cut brass, silver? Do mosaic

fountains pour jewelled
droplets, minute
domes quivering

on a pool's stony lip? In that moment,
you are again in the Seffarine Square,
surrounded

by the clang of leather-padded
hammers on metal
under the spreading plane

tree.
                    White ceramic,
glints,
lovely shards

splintered by time
and rough use.

                    White camellias,
soon to brown,

edges curling with age, clipped
chives, rosemary—can basil too
be for remembrance,

springing like mint in
hollow places?
Here rocks are the eggs

of dinosaurs, and blackberries—*Rosaceae
rubus*—thread the grasses, warp
to their weft. In Oregon, they call them

invasives. Unappreciated,
beautiful, this aggregate fruit,
dandelion seeds

                                    awaiting the wind.
When we steer through wire fencing,
pot holes, broken bottles,

the stubs of cigarettes, spires—
broken glass shoved into

concrete, wire,
wolf-welded. The roots
of trees lie corpulent,

                                    exposed.
These are our seraphic edifices, our
tape murals, these towers

that rise over the collapsed porches and
convulsed lintels

of Santa Ana and Seventh Street,
our cranium and lyre, our

                         sublime detritus.
Dandelions breathe their seeds into
heavy air, and they tangle in the branches

of oleander, shell petals
foam
                    afloat.

IV

Coda

Were There Gazelle

Sweep of my hair, wide expanse of savanna, a gazelle,
       neck long, legs extended

in flight as grass surges,
       whorls about hooves, slender legs.

Fading flanks, flash of hoof, men
       in the distance heave a carcass into a truck,

slanting sun turns swelling rib cage to gold.

The dogs slaver in the heat, dust the grass
       with glistening drops—and tears.

When there is no meat, a raven pecks corn,
       golden rain strewn across the fields.

In this spare harvest, she curbs her hunger for blood,
       lurches up to easy spirals, lungs tearing,

feathers speckled with earth,
       damp with the storm.

There is no shelter in folklore,
       and we taste what is to come

in what once was. These moments scour our passage,
       clear it of debris—of our human

discourse and rot—leave a few shining pebbles
       to bruise our feet.

Notes

Epigraph from Elena Johnson's "Edge Effect," from *Field Notes for the Alpine Tundra*. Gaspereau Press. Text Copyright © Elena Johnson, 2015. Used with the permission of Gaspereau Press.

The repeated line from "I listen to Istanbul" is inspired by Orhan Veli Kanik's poem, of the same name, originally in Turkish.

"Village in Kerala" includes a partial line from Alison Goodwin's poem "Crow Watching." *ARC Poetry Magazine 79*. Used with permission of the author.

"The Sun Casts No Shade" was inspired by a line from Angie Estes, "Pièta," from *Enchantée*. Oberlin College Press. Copyright © 2013 by Angie Estes. Used with permission of Oberlin College Press.

The title of "How to Know When the Dead are Dead" is from Angie Estes, excerpt from Estes, "How to Know When the Dead are Dead" from Estes's poem of the same name from *Enchantée*. Oberlin College Press. Copyright © 2013 by Angie Estes. Used with permission of Oberlin College Press.

"Atchafalaya Basin, Louisiana, May 1986" was inspired by a line from Andrea MacPherson's collection *Away*. Signature Editions, 2008. Used with permission of the author.

"Encounter" includes a line from Kate Cayley, excerpt from "Girl in a Checked Dress on a Slum Doorstep, 1912" in *When This World Comes to an End*. Brick Books. Copyright © 2013 by Kate Cayley. Used with permission of Brick Books.

"The Find" was inspired by a line from Kim Moore's chapbook *If We Could Speak Like Wolves*. Smith Doorstop, 2013. Used with permission of the author.

"Morning at Summer Palace, Beijing" was inspired by a line from Matt Miller's collection *Cameo Diner*. Loom Press, 2005. Used with permission of the author.

"I See China" was inspired by JMW Turner's painting "The Blue Rigi, Sunrise 1942."

"Ring of Brodgar, Orkney" includes a line from Natasha Trethewey, excerpt from Trethewey, "Storyville Diary: Disclosure" from *Bellocq's Ophelia*. Copyright © 2002 by Natasha Trethewey. Used with the permission of The Permissions Company, LLC on behalf of Graywolf Press, Minneapolis, Minnesota, www.graywolfpress.org.

"Village at Birsay" was inspired by a line from Phoebe Wang's poem "Career Path" from *Admission Requirements*. McClelland & Stewart, 2017. Used by permission of the author.

Acknowledgements

Sincere thanks to the editors and staff of *Blast Furnace, Clementine Poetry Journal, Grain Magazine, The Fiddlehead,* and S*ugared Water* in which some of these poems appeared previously in earlier versions.

Profound thanks to Caryl Peters of Frog Hollow Press who published an earlier version of "Distributaries" as a limited-edition chapbook.

My thanks as well to Robin Richardson who read an earlier version of "Bones of the Cathedral," and to Stuart Ross who read an early version of the manuscript in its entirety. Their commentary and suggestions greatly enhanced the work.

Many thanks to Jean Sheppard, my wonderful first reader, and to my husband, Michael Gemar, my best guide and critic.

My deepest gratitude to Monica Kidd, my superb editor at Pedlar Press, whose keen editorial eye and clear vision of the work and its possibilities have brought this collection far beyond what I could have imagined. Working with her has been a great pleasure and an incredible learning process.

Bio

Laura K. McRae is a teacher in Toronto, Ontario where she lives and writes. Her chapbook *Distributaries* was published in 2016 by Frog Hollow Press. *Were There Gazelle* is her first full-length collection.